SPIRIT OF THE
SHETLAND PONY

HEIDI M. SANDS

First published in Great Britain in 2010

British Library Cataloguing-in-Publication Data
A CIP record for this title is available from the British Library

ISBN 978 1 906887 59 9

PiXZ Books
Halsgrove House, Ryelands Industrial Estate,
Bagley Road, Wellington, Somerset TA21 9PZ
Tel: 01823 653777
Fax: 01823 216796
email: sales@halsgrove.com

An imprint of Halstar Ltd, part of the Halsgrove group of
companies
Information on all Halsgrove titles is available at:
www.halsgrove.com

Printed and bound in China by Toppan Leefung Printing Ltd

Introduction

What can you say about the Shetland pony that hasn't already been said? Cute, cuddly, child's favourite, playmate and companion, the Shetland has it all at its little hooftips.

Standing inches high, when all our other native ponies stand hands, the Shetland has guts and drive, size never stops this little powerhouse. Whether in harness, flying along in a scurry competition or on a lead rein with the tiniest of child riders safely in the saddle this most northerly of Britain's native breeds never fails to impress.

Exported and bred all over the world the Shetland pony is one of the most recognisable. Coiffured for the showring, vying for the top awards at the prestigious Royal Highland Show he shows himself to the best of his ability, mane and tail flying, handlers exhibiting for all they are worth.

At home in any company the Shetland is to be found in fields and on studs across the UK, but he is of course most at home on his native isles. Pushing rugs aside he is winter's biggest ball of fluff, place your hand within his overcoat on the coldest of days and you have the perfect hand-warmer.

This tiny breed has the tiniest of foals and from standard sized black ponies to miniature coloureds, including the delicious sounding blue eyed creams, each new life is born to captivate and delight. Give your heart to a Shetland pony and you'll never get it back!

A good mane and forelock is important in summer to keep the flies away and in winter to keep a pony warm.

Opposite page:
It doesn't always follow that a foal will be the same colour as mum.

Let sleeping foals lie.

Opposite page:
A pony can be taught many things with training and patience.

The top of a pony's tail should be left as nature intended in order to keep out icy blasts of rain and snow.

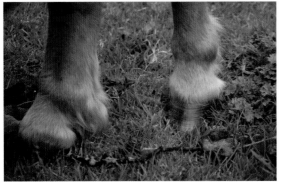

Tiny hooves like upturned coffee cups.

Eating thistles is not uncommon in spite of the prickles. Valuable nutrients are derived in this way. On their native scattald ponies will often eat seaweed.

A coloured line up.

Little and large
carry on camping.

Correct presentation for the judge is all important.

Opposite page:
A pretty pair of black ponies at the Royal Highland show.

Rowena Provan and Shetland
Pony Champion at the 2009 RHS
– Waulkmill Good Gracious.

Behind the scenes
at summer shows.

Judge Sonja Flaws from Sumburgh on Shetland giving her attention to a pony at the Black Isle Show in Ross Shire.

Show Champion stallion Kinkell Guardsman.

Opposite page:
Just following mum.

Just time for a quick bite to eat.

Making friends.

Trotting out in the grand parade.

It's sometimes difficult
to keep still in a line up.

Opposite page:
Beautiful just.

Ponies penned inside
the mart at Thainstone
in Aberdeenshire.

Summer shows often have
penning areas for ponies – here
a tiny foal takes a rest.

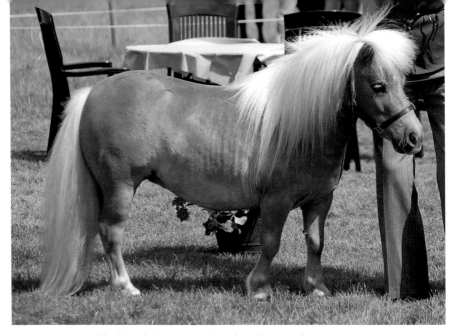

The breed throws some lovely colour combinations.
Opposite page:
The business of showing can turn into more of a gathering of friends.

Smartly turned out handlers complement their charges.

Young competitors are always encouraged in the showring.

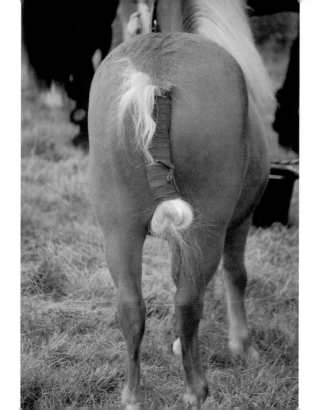

How to keep
your tail clean.

Opposite page:
I wonder what's
under here.

Ponies give confidence to child riders.

Opposite page:
Shetlands make great children's ponies.

Sometimes ponies and riders need helpers as here at Newtonmore in the Highlands.

What the best dressed
Shetland is wearing this season.

Waiting for his turn
in the showring.

Even foals groom themselves.

Opposite page:
It takes a lot of effort and rugs to keep a pony clean.

Driving is popular within the breed.

Opposite page:
A solid bay coloured pony with his skewbald friend.

A standard black foal not far from weaning age
ends the summer on a high with his mother.

As pretty as a picture, the breed is certainly eye catching.

How do I get out of here?

Opposite page:
In several inches of
snow a rug and a friend
are good allies.

In a field of
golden buttercups.

Opposite page:
Making the most of late
summer sunshine this
stallion lifted his head
to watch the camera.

Resting in the sun.

Opposite page:
Part of the Kellas herd foddering in the rain.

It's a delicate operation using your back hoof to scratch your face.

Opposite page: Manes and tails can catch the wind. On their native isles ponies are often blasted by winter storms and gales.

Out in the heather.

Opposite page:
Shetlands are good
doers which means
they can thrive where
others would fail.

Ponies will dig down through the snow to forage.

Opposite page:
Two friends wintering out in the snow.

Many different coat colours are found in the breed.

Opposite page:
Waiting at the gate.

Shetland ponies make great companions for other animals.

Opposite page:
Young foals prefer to stay close to mum.

So much mane on one so small.

Opposite page:
Small enough to find shelter behind a hedge.

Something caught this foal's attention at Grantown Show not far from Aviemore.

Opposite page: Teatime.

The escape artist.

Opposite page:
The Shetland pony, Scotland's smallest native breed.

With a flick of its tail a pony swats flies.

Opposite page:
Time for a feed.

Winnie Anderson's all black team vie for a feed.